Christmas '96.

From: Ande

Love Ya!

PROVERBIAL WISDOM

*A Treasury
of the
World's Greatest
Proverbs*

Robert Masello

CB

CONTEMPORARY
BOOKS

CHICAGO

Library of Congress Cataloging-in-Publication Data

    Proverbial wisdom : a treasury of the world's greatest proverbs / (compiled by) Robert Masello.   p. cm.
   ISBN 0-8092-3769-5
   I. Masello, Robert.
PN6405.P68   1993
398.9—dc20

                                 93-19859
                                     CIP

Published by Contemporary Books, Inc.
Two Prudential Plaza, Chicago, Illinois 60601-6790
Manufactured in the United States of America
International Standard Book Number: 0-8092-3769-5
10   9   8   7   6   5   4   3   2   1

Contents

Introduction

No matter where in the world you go—to a fishing village in the South Seas, a mining town in the north of England, a mountaintop aerie in Tibet, a desert oasis—the one thing you'll find is wisdom. It won't be on sale in the town market, and it won't be on display in the central square. But it will be available to anyone who listens to the local people—and their proverbs.

Proverbs are the distilled wisdom of the people who have created them. Lord Bacon described them as "the genius, wit, and spirit of a nation." Cervantes called a proverb a "short sentence drawn from long experience." And for all of us who use them ourselves in everyday speech—"One bad apple spoils the bunch," "A

bird in the hand is worth two in the bush,"
"Look before you leap"—they're a sort of
conversational shorthand, a quick and easy way
of underscoring a point or getting to the
bottom line.

In researching this book and compiling the
1,001 proverbs contained herein, I was struck
by a number of things—some inspiring, some
surprising. First of all, nobody—anywhere—had
a good word to say about lawyers. Oh, there
were plenty of proverbs about lawyers, but they
weren't what you'd call complimentary. To the
legal community at large, all I can say is,
"Sorry." And, by the way, you might want to
rethink your fee schedule.

Another thing I noticed was that proverbs, by
their very nature, tend to fall into fairly broad
categories, such as good and evil, poverty and
wealth, wisdom and folly. However unusual
their particular imagery might be, proverbs deal
in the big questions, the ones that people have
wrestled with for centuries. I've arranged the
chapters of this book around those same big
issues.

And finally, I was amazed to discover, time
and again, that the same proverbs, or very close
cousins, show up all over the world in what are
otherwise the most removed and dissimilar
cultures. The Italians might say "Rome wasn't

built in a day," but the French say the same of Paris, and the Russians make the same observation about Moscow. The English might advise, "Don't count your chickens before they're hatched," but the Danes say, "Don't sell the hide before you've caught the fox," and the Turks "You cannot sell the fish that are still in the sea." And while we might casually observe that "It's an ill wind that blows nobody good," in India they might say "When one man's house burns, another man may warm himself at the fire"; in west Africa, they believe that "What is bad luck for one man is good luck for another."

In *Proverbial Wisdom*, I've included sayings from at least fifty countries, and if there's one lesson to be learned from this book it's that there is indeed a family of man—for all the differences in color and custom, history and faith, people all over the world share feelings and beliefs and, yes, even jokes. And all of these are expressed—with concision, wit, and unparalleled vigor—in their proverbs.

For my brothers Steven and David,
who had nothing to do with this book.
I just thought I'd say hi.

On Love, Lust, and the Pursuit of Beauty

Love laughs at locksmiths.

❧ *America*

Love is like a mousetrap—you go in when you wish, but you don't come out when you like.

❧ *Spain*

Better to be off with the old love before we be on with the new.

❧ *Scotland*

Love lives in cottages as well as courts.

❧ *England*

It's as difficult to win love as to wrap salt in pine needles.

✤ *America*

A bachelor is never sent as a go-between.

✤ *Russia*

Loving and singing are not to be forced.

✤ *Germany*

An old man in love is like a flower in winter.

✤ *Portugal*

A man in love schemes more than a hundred lawyers.

✤ *Spain*

You can't force anyone to love you or to lend you money.

✤ *Jewish*

Men and women are never placed too far apart to be near.

✤ *Japan*

We always return to our first loves.
         ❧ *America*

One grows used to love and to fire.
         ❧ *France*

When two are in love, only one need eat.
         ❧ *Spain*

Beauty is a good letter of introduction.
         ❧ *Germany*

A maid that laughs is half taken.
         ❧ *England*

There is a road from heart to heart.
         ❧ *America*

Beauty may have fair leaves but bitter fruit.
         ❧ *England*

Words draw the nails from the heart.
         ❧ *Armenia*

A man is like a bear—the uglier he is, the more magnificent.

❧ *Spain*

Roasted cabbage tree during the day, and the pleasure of a woman during the night.

❧ *Maori*

Lovers' purses are tied with cobwebs.

❧ *Italy*

A man chases a woman until she catches him.

❧ *America*

He who has love in his heart has spurs in his sides.

❧ *England*

Love is like butter—it's good with bread.

❧ *Yiddish*

If you fall in love let her be a beauty; if you should steal, let it be a camel.

❧ *Lebanon*

A dog's nose and a maid's knees are always cold.

❧ America

She who loves an ugly man thinks him handsome.

❧ Spain

They that love most speak least.

❧ Scotland

A fine girl and a tattered gown always find something to hook them.

❧ France

Fire in the heart sends smoke into the head.

❧ Germany

The eyes have one language everywhere.

❧ Romania

It is easier to watch over one hundred fleas than one young girl.

❧ Poland

A man's heart changes as often as the
autumn sky.

✤ *Japan*

Better an honest smack in the face than a
false kiss.

✤ *Jewish*

A woman that likes to be at the window is like
a bunch of grapes on the highway.

✤ *England*

A handsome man will not be sought after, but
even a plain woman will be run after eagerly.

✤ *Maori*

Old love does not rust.

✤ *Estonia*

Do not sigh for him, but send for him; if he be
unhanged, he will come.

✤ *Scotland*

Poverty makes thieves, love makes poets.
❧ Japan

If you flatter the mother, you will hug the daughter.
❧ Russia

Faint heart never won fair lady.
❧ America

Love is a sweet dream, and marriage is the alarm clock.
❧ Jewish

On Friends, Enemies, and How to Tell the Two Apart

When a friend asks, there is no tomorrow.
❧ *Spain*

A friend you get for nothing; an enemy must be bought.
❧ *Yiddish*

Friends are one soul in two bodies.
❧ *Turkey*

If you want to know who your friends are, lie by the roadside and pretend to be drunk.
❧ *Jamaica*

A hedge between keeps friendship green.

🌿 *Germany*

It is more disgraceful to suspect our friends than to be deceived by them.

🌿 *France*

To a friend's house the road is never long.

🌿 *Denmark*

A false friend and a shadow attend only when the sun shines.

🌿 *America*

Every ten years one man has need of another.

🌿 *Italy*

Love your enemy—but don't put a gun in his hand.

🌿 *America*

All are not friends that speak us fair.

🌿 *Scotland*

He who gossips to you will gossip about you.

❧ *Lebanon*

Better to have a friend on the road than gold and silver in your purse.

❧ *France*

What a man thinks up for himself, his worst enemy couldn't wish for him.

❧ *Yiddish*

He who looks for a friend without a fault will never find one.

❧ *Armenia*

One who seeks no friends is his own enemy.

❧ *Russia*

Give your friend a pig and your enemy a peach.

❧ *Italy*

Never trust overmuch to a new friend or an old enemy.

❧ *Scotland*

The best friends are in one's purse.

❧ *Germany*

Make friends when you don't need them.

❧ *Jamaica*

Tell your secret to your friend and he will set
his foot upon your neck.

❧ *Italy*

Both your friend and your enemy think that you
will never die.

❧ *Ireland*

Never buy a horse from an enemy—it may have
some strange tricks.

❧ *Spain*

A friend to all is a friend to none.

❧ *Scotland*

He who lends to a friend loses doubly.

❧ *France*

One old friend is better than two new ones.
❦ *Yiddish*

Beware of a reconciled friend as of the devil.
❦ *Spain*

To preserve friendship, one must build walls.
❦ *Italy*

Rather lose your joke than lose your friend.
❦ *Scotland*

One may live without one's friend, but not without one's pipe.
❦ *Ireland*

Sudden friendship, sure repentance.
❦ *England*

Dine with a friend but do not do business with him.
❦ *Armenia*

Be a friend to yourself, and others will.

❧ *Scotland*

Tell your friend a lie—and if he keeps it a secret, tell him the truth.

❧ *Spain*

He who is the judge between two friends loses one of them.

❧ *Germany*

When friends meet, hearts warm.

❧ *Scotland*

When your enemy falls, don't rejoice—but don't pick him up either.

❧ *Yiddish*

Friends and mules fail us at hard passes.

❧ *Portugal*

One enemy is too much, and a hundred friends are not enough.

❧ *Italy*

When friendship goes with love it must play second fiddle.

❧ *Germany*

Be slow in choosing a friend, but slower in changing him.

❧ *Scotland*

Better to have one thousand enemies outside the house than to have one single enemy inside it.

❧ *Lebanon*

As mills require two stones, so friendship requires two heads.

❧ *Armenia*

A good friend is often better than a brother.

❧ *Yiddish*

Lend your money and lose your friend.

❧ *Scotland*

In the mirror everybody sees his best friend.

❧ *Yiddish*

He is a friend at sneezing time—the most that can be gotten from him is a "God bless you."

💠 Italy

Avoid a friend who covers you with his wings and destroys you with his beak.

💠 Spain

The friend who does not help me and the enemy who does not injure me make up a pair of earrings.

💠 Armenia

I would rather have a dog my friend than enemy.

💠 Germany

Can't I be your friend but I must be your fool, too?

💠 England

He that would have many friends should try a few of them.

💠 Italy

He is no friend who eats his own by himself,
and mine with me.

Portugal

Friends are like fiddle strings—they must not
be screwed too tight.

England

If you see your enemy in the sun, light some
more fires near him.

Hausa (Africa)

Let him who is wretched and beggared try
everybody and then his friends.

Italy

When friendship has a rent, there is no reel of
cotton that can mend it.

Russia

The coldness of a friend and the coldness of
linen—they never lasted long.

Scotland

May God not prosper our friends that they forget us.

❧ Spain

The friendship of a great man is like the shadow of a bush—soon gone.

❧ France

An untried friend is like an uncracked nut.

❧ Russia

Trust not the praise of a friend nor the contempt of an enemy.

❧ Italy

There is no need like the lack of a friend.

❧ Ireland

Friendship is a plant which one must often water.

❧ Germany

An old friend is a mount for a black day.

❧ Turkey

A ready way to lose your friend is to lend
him money.

❧ *England*

Without a bright mirror a woman cannot tell if
the powder is smooth on her face; without a
true friend the intelligent man cannot tell when
he's made a mistake.

❧ *China*

Buy friendship with presents, and it will be
bought from you.

❧ *Scotland*

God keep me from my friends; from my enemies
I will keep myself.

❧ *Italy*

When good cheer is lacking, our friends will
be packing.

❧ *England*

On Bartering, Marketing, and Taking Care of Business

You will never know a man till you do business with him.

❧ *Scotland*

Partnership is an invention of the devil.

❧ *Russia*

A carpenter is known by his chips.

❧ *Romania*

If you would not be cheated, ask the price at three shops.

❧ *China*

He who trusts you with his throat, cut it not.

❧ *Lebanon*

Buy from desperate people, and sell to newlyweds.

❧ *Spain*

Do not sell sun in July.

❧ *Italy*

Better to have friends in the marketplace than money in your coffers.

❧ *Portugal*

There are more foolish buyers than foolish sellers.

❧ *France*

One never tires working for oneself.

❧ *Russia*

Were I a hatter, men would come into the world without heads.

❧ *Germany*

Opportunity makes the thief.

❧ *Italy*

The work praises the man.

❧ *Ireland*

Good wares make a quick market.

❧ *Scotland*

Customers are jade, merchandise is grass.

❧ *China*

Buying is cheaper than asking.

❧ *Germany*

For the buyer a hundred eyes are too few; for the seller one is enough.

❧ *Italy*

A dealer in onions is a good judge of scallions.

❧ *France*

The customer's always right.

❧ *America*

If I dealt in candles, the sun wouldn't set.

❦ Yiddish

If I were to trade in winding sheets, no one would die.

❦ Saudi Arabia

An honest man does not make himself a dog for the sake of a bone.

❦ Denmark

He who is meant to be a basket carrier is born with the handle in his hand.

❦ Italy

Bad merchandise is never cheap.

❦ France

Let them whip me in the marketplace, provided it be not known at home.

❦ Spain

Two women and a goose make a market.

❦ Italy

Three women, three geese, and three frogs
make a fair.

❧ *Germany*

Honesty is like an icicle—if once it melts, that's
the end of it.

❧ *America*

Take your son to the marketplace and see with
whom he associates.

❧ *Syria*

He who dispraises a thing wants to buy it.

❧ *France*

When fools go to market, peddlers make money.

❧ *Holland*

Approach the perfumer and thou wilt
be perfumed.

❧ *Hebrew*

Would you shear a donkey for wool?

❧ *Latin*

He who cannot speak well of his trade does not understand it.

❧ France

Every peddler praises his own pot and more if it is cracked.

❧ Spain

He who owns even one ear of the camel has the right to make it kneel on the ground.

❧ Lebanon

If I am seen I am joking; if I am not seen I steal.

❧ Germany

He who stands near the woodcutter is likely to be hit by a splinter.

❧ Denmark

The market is not anybody's home.

❧ Hausa (Africa)

Do not open a shop unless you like to smile.

❧ China

I hear the noise of the mill but see no flour.

    ❧ *Persia*

A workman is known by his work.

    ❧ *Holland*

The terrible calligrapher is choosy about
his brushes.

    ❧ *Korea*

The man of many trades begs his bread
on Sunday.

    ❧ *Romania*

At an auction keep your mouth shut.

    ❧ *Spain*

A single penny fairly got is worth a thousand
that are not.

    ❧ *Germany*

No melon peddler cries, "Bitter melons." No
wine dealer says, "Sour wine."

    ❧ *China*

In a deal there are two fools—the one who asks too much and the one who asks too little.

❧ *Russia*

If your head is made of butter, don't be a baker.

❧ *France*

In a soap maker's house, a person who doesn't fall, slips.

❧ *Spain*

Worry about what to buy—never worry about what to sell.

❧ *Lebanon*

One cry of "Thief!" and the whole marketplace is on the lookout.

❧ *Hausa (Africa)*

Creditors have better memories than debtors.

❧ *England*

The bad workman never finds a good tool.

❧ *France*

To open a shop is easy—the hard part is
keeping it open.

❧ *China*

He who does not teach his son a trade teaches
him to steal.

❧ *Hebrew*

The man who talks with the blacksmith gets hit
by sparks.

❧ *Kurdish*

No man is a master of his craft the first day.

❧ *Romania*

Go early to market and as late as you can
to battle.

❧ *Italy*

On Health and Medicine

The earth covers the doctor's mistakes.
❧ *Italy*

No man is a good physician who has never
been sick.
❧ *Saudi Arabia*

A lucky physician is better than a learned one.
❧ *Germany*

An imaginary illness is worse than a real one.
❧ *Yiddish*

Don't call in the doctor after the funeral.

❦ Japan

There's no physician like a true friend.

❦ Romania

God heals and the doctor has the thanks.

❦ Italy

The patient who names a doctor his heir makes a big mistake.

❦ Spain

Midday sun is the remedy for a cold.

❦ Hausa (Africa)

He that eats but one dish seldom needs the doctor.

❦ Scotland

The best physicians are Dr. Diet, Dr. Quiet, and Dr. Merryman.

❦ America

A wound never heals so well that a scar cannot be seen.

✤ Denmark

The last resort is the hot iron.

✤ Lebanon

When the sun comes in, the doctor goes out.

✤ England

It ill becomes a carpenter to be heavy-handed, a smith to be shaky-handed, or a physician to be tenderhearted.

✤ Scotland

Pay the doctor, praise the Lord.

✤ Jamaica

The tongue goes to where the tooth aches.

✤ France

Invalids live the longest.

✤ Japan

Illness comes in by mouth, and ills come out by it.

❧ China

A doctor and a clown know more than a doctor alone.

❧ Italy

A cool mouth and warm feet live long.

❧ England

The medicine that hurts the most is generally the best healer.

❧ Scotland

A bad wound may heal, but a bad name will kill.

❧ Scotland

A footache is forgotten, a headache not.

❧ Armenia

Make a plaster as large as the sore.

❧ England

What can't be cured must be endured.
England

Diseases are the visits of God.
Italy

Life is the biggest bargain—we get it for nothing!
Yiddish

Hussars pray for war and doctors for fever.
Germany

Doctors who ride chairs never ride them to hovels.
China

One foot is better than two crutches.
America

God feels the pulse and then prescribes the medicine.
Lebanon

Death is the poor man's doctor.

♣ Ireland

The sick man is free to say all.

♣ Italy

A dry cough is the trumpeter o' death.

♣ Scotland

Feed a cold and starve a fever.

♣ America

Two thirds of medicine is abstinence.

♣ Lebanon

There are more old drunkards than old doctors.

♣ France

Victims of the same disease have much to
talk about.

♣ Japan

A great doctor is accompanied by a great angel.
❦ *Yiddish*

Strong folks have strong maladies.
❦ *Germany*

If you have a friend who is a doctor, make your bow and send him to the house of your enemy.
❦ *Spain*

When I'm dead, everybody's dead—and the pig too.
❦ *Italy*

A man should stay alive if only out of curiosity.
❦ *Yiddish*

He who has not health has nothing.
❦ *France*

An old physician and a young lawyer are the best.
❦ *England*

Good medicine has often a bitter smack.
& *Japan*

Of the malady a man fears, he dies.
& *Spain*

Tender surgeons make foul wounds.
& *Holland*

He who is born with a weak intellect and a
goiter can never be cured.
& *Italy*

A boil is fine as long as it's under someone
else's arm.
& *Yiddish*

When Fate arrives, the physician becomes a fool.
& *Saudi Arabia*

No good doctor ever takes physic.
& *Italy*

Physicians are costly visitors.

✤ England

If you want to be dead, wash your head and go
to bed.

✤ Spain

Witch doctors do not sell their potions to
each other.

✤ Mozambique

Diet cures more than doctors.

✤ Scotland

Asking pardon doesn't cure the bump.

✤ Martinique

That city is in a bad state whose physician has
the gout.

✤ Hebrew

The doctor cannot drink medicine for
the patient.

✤ Germany

At the sight of death, man calls after the fever.

❧ *Armenia*

Fear kills more people than the physicians.

❧ *Spain*

Even honey can taste bitter if it's used
for medicine.

❧ *Korea*

Sickness comes on horseback and departs
on foot.

❧ *Holland*

A kick is like medicine to the crooked old man.

❧ *India (Kashmir)*

The house into which sunshine enters, no
physician enters.

❧ *Lebanon*

Your health comes first—you can always hang
yourself later.

❧ *Yiddish*

On Wealth and Poverty

The rich get richer, and the poor get babies.
     🌿 *America*

No one is poor but he who thinks himself so.
     🌿 *Portugal*

What makes you happy makes you rich.
     🌿 *Russia*

Poverty is no disgrace, but it's also no
great honor.
     🌿 *Yiddish*

When the sea turned into honey, the beggar lost his spoon.

❧ Bulgaria

I had rather ask of my fire brown bread than borrow of my neighbor white.

❧ Romania

The potter sleeps soundly, for no one would steal clay.

❧ India (Bihar)

Penny wise and pound foolish.

❧ Scotland

Better some of a pudding than none of a pie.

❧ England

Begged bread has a hard crust.

❧ Germany

Money is like down—one puff and it's gone.

❧ Russia

Poverty is even worse if you have to sleep on the edge of a crowded bed.

      ❧ *Spain*

The wealth of the wicked will be scattered by the wind like chaff.

      ❧ *Mozambique*

Poverty is the common fate of scholars.

      ❧ *China*

A beggar's wallet is a mile to the bottom.

      ❧ *Scotland*

The rich man has more relations than he knows.

      ❧ *France*

Don't invest your money on the advice of a poor man.

      ❧ *Spain*

Where poverty shows up first is in the face.

      ❧ *Yiddish*

My debtor is a worse payer even than I am.

         ❦ *Saudi Arabia*

The poor man seeks for food, the rich man
for appetite.

         ❦ *Denmark*

A fool may earn money, but it takes a wise man
to keep it.

         ❦ *Scotland*

Poverty is the reward of idleness.

         ❦ *Holland*

If you have money, you are wise and good
looking, and, my, how well you sing!

         ❦ *Yiddish*

If you cannot become rich, be the neighbor of a
rich man.

         ❦ *Armenia*

The rich man plans for tomorrow, the poor man for today.

❧ China

Better a poor horse than an empty stall.

❧ Denmark

He takes from St. Peter and gives to St. Paul.

❧ England

A debt of gold we can repay, but kindness indebts till our dying day.

❧ Malaysia

If I have lost the ring, I still have the fingers!

❧ Italy

If a poor man gives to you, he expects more in return.

❧ Portugal

Money is the best servant.

❧ India

If you eat your bagel, you'll have nothing in your pocket but the hole.

❧ Yiddish

It is a grief to one beggar that another stands at the door.

❧ Holland

Poverty is a sin that the rich never forgive.

❧ Russia

A stingy man is always poor.

❧ France

Slippery is the flagstone at the mansion-house door.

❧ Scotland

An ass covered with gold is more respected than a good horse with a pack saddle.

❧ England

Better poor on land than rich at sea.

❧ Holland

If a rich man dies, all the world is moved; if a poor one dies, nobody knows it.

❧ Armenia

In a fight the rich worry about their faces, while the poor worry about their pants.

❧ Russia

A heart free from care is better than a full purse.

❧ Saudi Arabia

Birds are caught with grains, men with money.

❧ Armenia

The poor man's enemies are few, the rich man's friends are even fewer.

❧ Yiddish

There never was a five-pound note but there was a ten-pound road for it.

❧ Scotland

He who giveth to the poor lendeth to the Lord.

❧ *Holland*

Better rags than nakedness.

❧ *Haiti*

God shares with the person who is generous.

❧ *Ireland*

Honesty makes rich, but she works slowly.

❧ *Germany*

He who has money can eat ice cream in hell.

❧ *Lebanon*

If you make yourself a dog, make yourself a rich man's dog.

❧ *Japan*

A beggar himself, can he afford to have one asking for alms at his door?

❧ *India (Bihar)*

The poorer, the more generous.

❧ *Russia*

Too much prosperity makes most men fools.

❧ *Italy*

Every poor man has a dry throat and wet boots.

❧ *Jewish*

Not even water would leak from his fist.

❧ *Malaysia*

Take care of the pence and the pounds will take care of themselves.

❧ *England*

There is a life of iron and a life of silver.

❧ *Armenia*

Money is better than my lord's letter.

❧ *Scotland*

He who would be rich in one year is hanged at the end of six months.

❧ *Italy*

Poverty is in want of much, avarice of everything.

❧ *Romania*

Poor people entertain with the heart.

❧ *Haiti*

God will provide—if only God would provide until He provides.

❧ *Yiddish*

If a rich man eats a snake people say, "This is wisdom!" If a poor man eats a snake people say, "This is foolishness!"

❧ *Lebanon*

Money is only good for a weekday, a holiday, and a rainy day.

❧ *Russia*

A slothful man is a beggar's brother.

✿ *Scotland*

If the rich could hire others to die for them, the poor could make a nice living.

✿ *Yiddish*

On Connubial Bliss . . .
and Burdens

More belongs to marriage than four bare legs
in a bed.

❧ *England*

Marriage has teeth, and him bite very hot.

❧ *Jamaica*

Never marry a widow unless her first husband
was hanged.

❧ *England*

A fat wife is like a blanket in winter.

❧ *Pakistan*

A deaf husband and a blind wife are always a happy couple.

❦ Denmark

Never take a wife till you know what to do with her.

❦ Scotland

One daughter helps to marry another.

❦ Italy

A wife and a pot get better as they get older.

❦ Japan

Before you marry, keep two eyes open; after you marry, shut one.

❦ Jamaica

In bed, husband and wife. Out of bed, guests.

❦ China

A man canna wive and thrive the same year.

❦ Scotland

Gentlemen prefer blonds—but marry brunets.

✤ America

There is nothing better than a rich wife and a generous mother-in-law.

✤ Russia

A husband is not a flower with which to decorate your head.

✤ Lebanon

'Tis dangerous marrying a widow, because she has cast her rider.

✤ England

If an old wife won't do for a jar, she'll do for a lid.

✤ Spain

A rich man's wooing need seldom be a long one.

✤ Scotland

A woman and a melon are hard to choose.

❧ France

Better be a cuckold and not know it than be none and everybody say so.

❧ Scotland

If marriages are made in heaven, you two have few friends there.

❧ Scotland

To kill only one iguana is a shame for the hunter; but a man who marries four wives is praised in the land.

❧ Mozambique

A mill and a wife are always in want of something.

❧ Italy

A young wife is an old man's post-horse to the grave.

❧ Germany

Love does wonders, but money makes
marriages.

❧ France

Better half hang'd than ill married.

❧ Scotland

Her husband is a leg of a chair.

❧ Lebanon

Marriage is not a race—you can always get
there in time.

❧ Russia

Borrowed wives, like borrowed books, are
seldom returned.

❧ America

Choose cloth by its edge; a wife, by her mother.

❧ Persia

Handsome women generally fall to the lot of
ugly men.

❧ Italy

Choose the good mother's daughter, were the Devil her father.

♣ *Scotland*

She who is born handsome is born married.

♣ *England*

The weeping bride makes a laughing wife.

♣ *Germany*

The man has neither sense nor reason who leaves a young wife at home.

♣ *France*

Married folk are like rats in a trap—fain to get others in, but fain to be out themselves.

♣ *Scotland*

A beautiful wife without money is like a fine house without furniture.

♣ *Spain*

Pick your wife in the kitchen.

♣ *Japan*

He drives a good wagonload into his farm that gets a good wife.

Scotland

Lying will marry you a wife, but it won't keep her.

Fulani (Africa)

He has most share in the wedding that lies with the bride.

England

Marry your cousin, so that if evil comes it will be kept to yourself.

Maori

He that would have a beautiful wife should choose her on a Saturday.

Spain

The matchmaker gets three cups of wine when he succeeds and three slaps on the cheek when he fails.

Korea

Marry your son when you please, your daughter
when you can.

❧ *France*

Every one sings as he has the gift, and marries
as he has the luck.

❧ *Portugal*

When a poor man makes a wedding, the dog
gets the shivers!

❧ *Yiddish*

He that marries for wealth sells his liberty.

❧ *England*

Fortune gains the bride.

❧ *Scotland*

He who takes a wife takes a master.

❧ *France*

Marry a man with blistered hands.

❧ *Maori*

A man without a wife is like a man in winter
without a fur hat.

♣ Russia

A man who's too good for the world is no good
to his wife.

♣ Yiddish

He who makes a bad marriage never escapes
from his troubles.

♣ Italy

A bonnie bride's soon adorned.

♣ Scotland

All is well, for if the bride has not fair hair, she
has a fair skin.

♣ Holland

A man cannot marry if he doesn't possess
any cashews.

♣ Jamaica

Old wives are good indeed to wed—the mind is schooled and stomach fed.

❧ *Malaysia*

Choose your wife with her nightcap on.

❧ *Scotland*

The couple's quarrel and the west wind die down at dark.

❧ *Japan*

A rakish bachelor makes a jealous husband.

❧ *Italy*

A dish o' married love soon grows cold.

❧ *Scotland*

Husband and wife in perfect concord are like the music of the harp and lute.

❧ *China*

Marry for love and work for silver.

❧ *Scotland*

Leave her now and then if you would really love
your wife.

❧ *Malaysia*

Marry a poor woman. It is God who shall make
you rich.

❧ *Lebanon*

He who marries for love has good nights and
bad days.

❧ *France*

Don't marry without love, but don't love
without reason.

❧ *America*

The heart is the treasury of the tongue.

❧ *Saudi Arabia*

He that marries a widow will have a dead man's
head often thrown in his dish.

❧ *Scotland*

Even a dog does not eat a marital quarrel.

❧ *Japan*

A sad bride makes a glad wife.

❧ *Holland*

There is a mate even for an old straw shoe.

❧ *Korea*

Good-Enough has got a wife and Far-Better wants.

❧ *Scotland*

Many a good hanging prevents a bad marriage.

❧ *America*

On Family Values and Family Politics

Where there is room in the heart, there is room in the house.

❧ *Denmark*

As the old bird sings, so the young ones twitter.

❧ *Germany*

Don't blame your wife's side if your son is cross-eyed.

❧ *Russia*

'Tis a bad house that has not an old man in it.

❧ *Italy*

Neither the child that is unchastised nor the moustache that is untwirled will be right.

❧ *India*

Rear sons for old age, and store grain against famine.

❧ *China*

There's no advice like father's—even if you don't take it.

❧ *America*

Mules make a great fuss about their ancestors having been horses.

❧ *Germany*

What children hear their parents say by the fireside, they repeat in the highway.

❧ *Spain*

One father can support ten children, but it is difficult for ten children to support one father.

❧ *Yiddish*

Whatever your uncle gives you, take.
❧ *Lebanon*

He that is born of a hen must scrape for
a living.
❧ *England*

If you love your son, make him leave home.
❧ *Japan*

Our neighbor's children are always the worst.
❧ *Germany*

Bathe other people's children, but don't wash
behind their ears.
❧ *Trinidad*

The hand that rocks the cradle rules the world.
❧ *Scotland*

The rope dancer's son is always turning
somersaults.
❧ *India*

The teeth of the puppy are growing while the old dog is gnawing bones.
❧ Denmark

The husband's mother is the wife's devil.
❧ Germany

The preacher's sons always turn out badly.
❧ America

A wild goose never laid a tame egg.
❧ Ireland

He who singles out one child and gives him even one more date than he gives his other children, God shall single him out by giving him a piece of glowing coal.
❧ Lebanon

Lay hold of the words your father gives you.
❧ Maori

To drunken mothers-in-law give brimming jugs.
❧ Spain

Bring up a raven and he will peck out
your eyes.

❧ France

A small child hurts your knee; a grown child
hurts your heart.

❧ Russia

The day your horse dies and your money's gone,
your relatives change to strangers.

❧ China

Mother-in-law and daughter-in-law, storm
and hail.

❧ Italy

Hit a child and quarrel with its mother.

❧ Hausa (Africa)

Children are the riches of the poor.

❧ Denmark

Ragged colts make the handsomest stallions.

❧ Germany

If ye had as little money as ye have manners, ye would be the poorest man of all your kin.

& *Scotland*

The porcupine says, "Oh, my soft little son, softer than butter," and the crow says, "My son, whiter than muslin."

& *Afghanistan*

Better to have something yourself than to beg of your sister.

& *Denmark*

Eagles do not breed doves.

& *Germany*

It is easy to govern a kingdom but difficult to rule one's family.

& *China*

The father wore a mallet about his neck, the son a precious necklace.

& *Italy*

With a child in the house, all corners are full.
❧ *Yiddish*

Though your own kinsmen may chew you, they will not swallow you.
❧ *Lebanon*

If the father is a fisherman, the children look into the water.
❧ *Russia*

If my aunt had wheels, she might be an omnibus.
❧ *Holland*

It is a sorry house in which the cock is silent and the hen crows.
❧ *France*

Of brothers-in-law and red dogs, few are good.
❧ *Spain*

There is no such thing as a bad mother.
❧ *Yiddish*

If the old wife hadna been in the oven, she ne'er would hae thought o' seeking her daughter there.

❧ *Scotland*

A bad son and a bad coin will save you sometime or other.

❧ *India*

Every man thinks his own owl a falcon.

❧ *Holland*

The house with an old grandparent harbors a jewel.

❧ *China*

Massage the legs of your daughter, that she may have a good appearance when standing before the fire on the beach.

❧ *Maori*

Call a grocer father and he will give sugar.

❧ *India*

The monkey smothers its young one by hugging it too much.

❧ *Martinique*

Bringing up boys is like cracking flint with one's teeth.

❧ *Lebanon*

The chimney is crooked, but the smoke rises straight.

❧ *Armenia*

He who is on horseback no longer knows his own father.

❧ *Russia*

Flesh will warm to kin, even against a man's will.

❧ *Scotland*

The tree must be bent while it is young.

❧ *Germany*

When a father praises his son, he flatters
himself.

❧ *America*

They're scarce of news who speak ill of
their mother.

❧ *Ireland*

He to whom God gives no sons, the devil
gives nephews.

❧ *Spain*

The mother a radish, the father an onion, and
the son a saffron flower.

❧ *India*

To understand your parents' love you must raise
children yourself.

❧ *China*

He who marries a widow with three children
marries four thieves.

❧ *Denmark*

The pumpkin vine never bears watermelons.

❧ Creole (Belize)

Youth sheds many a skin.

❧ Ireland

A spoiled son becomes a gambler, while a spoiled daughter becomes a harlot.

❧ India

Brothers are like hands and feet.

❧ China

He that hath no children doth bring them up well.

❧ England

Praise the young and they will blossom.

❧ Ireland

Some families are like potatoes—all that's good of them is underground.

❧ America

On Domestic Duties, Delights, and Diversions

Marrying is easy, but housekeeping is hard.
❧ *Germany*

Were everyone to sweep before his own house, every street would be clean.
❧ *Holland*

A new broom sweeps clean.
❧ *Italy*

A new broom sweeps clean, but the old brush knows the corners.
❧ *Ireland*

Better repair the gutter than the whole house.

❧ *Portugal*

A single log doesn't warm the fireplace.

❧ *Yiddish*

When you put your hand in your own flour
barrel, you put it in to the wrist; but when you
put it in your neighbor's, you put it in to the
elbow.

❧ *Jamaica*

He that peeks through a keyhole may see what
will vex him.

❧ *Scotland*

Don't praise your furnace when the house
is cold.

❧ *Russia*

When you are thirsty, it's too late to think of
digging the well.

❧ *Japan*

A new pot keeps the water cold for a few days.

❧ Persia

All that's said in the kitchen should not be told in the hall.

❧ Scotland

How easily a hair gets into the butter.

❧ Germany

Old ovens are soon hot.

❧ England

A scabby head fears the comb.

❧ Holland

Loaves put into the oven awry come out crooked.

❧ France

One of the greatest labor-saving inventions of today is tomorrow.

❧ America

When you go to your neighbor's, you find out what is happening at home.

❧ *Yiddish*

Charity begins at home but shouldna end there.

❧ *Scotland*

Whoever frequents the kitchen smells of smoke.

❧ *Italy*

The day I did not sweep the house, there came to it one I did not expect.

❧ *Spain*

To every bird, its own nest seems fair.

❧ *France*

It is no time to play chess when the house is on fire.

❧ *Italy*

Stretch your legs according to your coverlet.

❧ *England*

Let everyone sweep before his own door.

✤ *Germany*

When the guest coughs, he's lacking a spoon.

✤ *Yiddish*

Peace and a well-built house cannot be bought too dearly.

✤ *Denmark*

Dirty linen should be washed at home.

✤ *France*

Don't wrestle with a curtain.

✤ *Japan*

The smoke of my own house is better than another man's fire.

✤ *Italy*

The lovelorn cook oversalts the porridge.

✤ *Germany*

Let him who is cold blow the fire.

❧ France

He that would keep his house clean must not let priest or pigeon into it.

❧ France

One hour's sleep before midnight is better than two after.

❧ Germany

It is a lonely washing that has no man's shirt in it.

❧ Ireland

They that live in glass houses should not throw stones.

❧ England

A clear conscience is a good pillow.

❧ France

A lazy boy and a warm bed are hard to part.

❧ Denmark

When the cook and the steward fall out, we hear who stole the butter.

❧ Holland

A big blanket makes a man sleep late.

❧ Jamaica

Insects do not nest in a busy door hinge.

❧ China

He who buys a house gets many a plank and nail for nothing.

❧ Germany

Sour wine, old bacon, and rye bread keep a house rich.

❧ Spain

A house without a dog, a cat, or a little child is a house without joy or laughter.

❧ Scotland

A single post can't hold up a sagging house.

❧ Japan

On Wining and Dining, Feasts and Famine

Enough's as good as a feast.

❧ *Scotland*

The fox says of the mulberries when he cannot get at them, "They are not good at all."

❧ *France*

He who likes drinking is always talking of wine.

❧ *Italy*

If you sing before breakfast, you'll cry before night.

❧ *America*

A good meal is worth hanging for.

❧ Germany

Bonnie cooks never made good broth.

❧ Scotland

In the end it will be known who ate the bacon.

❧ France

He's like a bagpipe—you never hear him till his belly's full.

❧ England

Live not to eat, but eat to live.

❧ Scotland

Better that you should be made to wait for food than that food should be made to wait for you.

❧ Hausa (Africa)

He who wants to eat honey should bear the stings of bees.

❧ Lebanon

When eating bamboo sprouts, remember the man who planted them.

❧ *China*

There was a wife who kept her supper for her breakfast, and she was dead before day.

❧ *England*

A hungry man smells meat far.

❧ *Scotland*

Good wine makes good blood.

❧ *Italy*

A good stew can't be made with water alone.

❧ *Spain*

Better to cross an angry man than a fasting one.

❧ *Denmark*

It is his feast, and he gets broken bits of cake!

❧ *India (Bihar)*

A man who has no knife cannot eat pineapple.
❧ *Jamaica*

Fair words don't butter the cabbage.
❧ *Germany*

The way to a man's heart is through his stomach.
❧ *America*

Much meat, much maladies.
❧ *England*

He who has been burnt by the hot blows even upon the cold.
❧ *Greece*

Every dog knows his dinnertime.
❧ *Jamaica*

When a poor man gets to eat a chicken, one of them is sick.
❧ *Yiddish*

It is better to have a piece of bread and an onion in peace than to have a stuffed lamb with quarrels.

❧ Lebanon

Hunger is the best sauce.

❧ France

Let us hurry and finish up the food; when visitors arrive, the meal will be over.

❧ Maori

There's many a slip twixt the cup and the lip.

❧ England

If you eat it up at supper, you cannot have it at breakfast.

❧ Spain

A little pepper burns a big man's mouth.

❧ Jamaica

The shorter the dinner, the longer the life.

❧ Russia

The patient man cooks a stone till he drinks
broth from it.

❧ Hausa (Africa)

A mouthful more does not pierce the belly.

❧ Armenia

You can't fill your belly painting pictures
of bread.

❧ China

Cheese is gold in the morning, silver at noon,
and lead at night.

❧ Germany

Brandy is lead in the morning, silver at noon,
and gold at night.

❧ Germany

When wine enters, modesty departs.

❧ Italy

He who mixes himself with bran will be eaten
by the chickens.

❧ Lebanon

Even the diamond mountains must be seen on a
full stomach.

❧ Korea

Drink even water at a tavern and you are
suspected of having drunk spirits.

❧ India

To a good cat, a good rat.

❧ France

Your head's nae sooner up than your
stomach's yappin'.

❧ Scotland

He who has no thirst has no business at
the fountain.

❧ Holland

The bigger the fish, the more butter it takes.

❧ Jamaica

The first dish pleases everyone.

❧ Italy

If a man quarrels with corn, hunger will
kill him.

❧ Hausa (Africa)

The choicest meal does not satisfy the glutton.

❧ Armenia

The drunken mouth reveals the heart's secrets.

❧ Germany

A good dog never gets a good bone.

❧ France

What is sweet in the mouth is not always good
in the stomach.

❧ Denmark

The nearer the bone, the sweeter the meat.

❧ Jamaica

When everybody says you are drunk, go
to sleep.

            ❧ *Italy*

Good wine needs no sign.

            ❧ *France*

If it rained macaroni, what a fine time
for gluttons!

            ❧ *Italy*

To one who has a pie in the oven, you may give
a bit of your cake.

            ❧ *France*

Worries are easier to bear with soup than
without it.

            ❧ *Yiddish*

It is better to have bread left over than to run
short of wine.

            ❧ *Spain*

The cask always smells of the herring.
❧ France

He can get seven bites out of one raisin.
❧ Armenia

Even food can attack.
❧ Maori

Whatever is in the pot will of course come into the ladle.
❧ India

Even the best of cooks will sooner or later drop a whole tomato.
❧ Spain

After meat comes mustard.
❧ Holland

Acorns were good till bread was found.
❧ America

A trout in the pot is better than a salmon in the pool.

❧ *Ireland*

Since the wine is drawn, it must be drunk.

❧ *France*

If you want your dinner, don't insult the cook.

❧ *China*

What is this fast? What is this pickled cabbage? Why do you talk about fasting while eating?

❧ *Turkey*

To sleep without dinner is better than to wake up in debt.

❧ *Jamaica*

Froth is no beer.

❧ *Holland*

I've fried my sausage in better pans than these.

❧ *Spain*

Don't refuse a wing to the one who gave you the chicken.

❧ Spain

Go home when the table is set and to church when the service is almost over.

❧ Armenia

He that is ashamed to eat is ashamed to live.

❧ France

You cannot have your cake and eat it too.

❧ England

Eggs and oaths are easily broken.

❧ Denmark

Always rise from the table with an appetite and you'll never sit down without one.

❧ America

A cheerful look makes a dish a feast.

❧ Romania

He has licked the butter off my bread.

♣ *Scotland*

A drink precedes a story.

♣ *Ireland*

When you eat garlic, it speaks for itself.

♣ *Russia*

Nature gave us two cheeks instead of one to make it easier to eat hot food.

♣ *Ghana*

A man who eats in the dark sometimes eats a cockroach in his supper.

♣ *Jamaica*

Eat till ye sweat and work till ye freeze.

♣ *Scotland*

Without bread and wine, even love will pine.

♣ *France*

Every meal is a lesson learned.

          ❧ *England*

If you're not done eating, don't throw away your plate.

          ❧ *Jamaica*

Drink and frankfurters for a dime kill a man before his time.

          ❧ *America*

On Good and Evil

The road to ruin is paved with good intentions.
❧ *Germany*

He begins to grow bad who believes
himself good.
❧ *Italy*

You don't have to die—heaven and hell are in
this world too.
❧ *Japan*

Tell everybody your business and the devil will
do it for you.
❧ *Italy*

Both the cross and the gallows are made
of wood.

❧ Poland

Eat with the devil, but give him a long spoon.

❧ Jamaica

Sufficient for the day is the evil thereof.

❧ France

A pack of cards is the devil's prayer book.

❧ Germany

Hold to the bad luck you have lest you
get worse.

❧ Lebanon

Where the devil cannot put his head he puts
his tail.

❧ Italy

When the Devil finds the door is shut, he
goes away.

❧ France

One good turn deserves another.

❧ *France*

A good heart breaks bad fortune.

❧ *Spain*

The devil never sent a wind out of Hell but he sailed with it.

❧ *Scotland*

A word can help a good person, but even a stick can't help the bad.

❧ *Yiddish*

If the Devil were dead, folk would do little for God's sake.

❧ *Scotland*

A kind word never broke anyone's mouth.

❧ *Ireland*

Let the devil get into the church, and he will mount the altar.

❧ *Germany*

Good repute is like the cypress—once cut, it never puts forth leaf again.

❧ Italy

Scandal is like an egg—when hatched, it has wings.

❧ Russia

In the day of prosperity, be agreeable; in the day of evil, be evil.

❧ Maori

He who does not punish evil invites it.

❧ Germany

The Devil's a busy bishop in his own diocese.

❧ Scotland

If God were living on earth, people would break His windows.

❧ Yiddish

Heaven is only three feet above your head.

❧ China

Curses are like processions—they return to the place they started out from.

❧ *Italy*

The smith's dog sleeps at the noise of the hammer and wakes at the grinding of teeth.

❧ *Spain*

Where God builds a church, the devil builds a chapel.

❧ *Germany*

Do good and throw it into the sea—if it is not appreciated by ungrateful man, it will be appreciated by God.

❧ *Lebanon*

When your devil was born, mine was going to school.

❧ *Italy*

Gold and goods may be lost—a good name endures forever.

❧ *Germany*

An idle man is the devil's pillow.
♣ Holland

A wicked tongue is worse than an evil hand.
♣ Yiddish

The bad man always suspects knavery.
♣ Spain

Good and bad make up a city.
♣ Portugal

The parson christens his own child first.
♣ Creole (Belize)

A nickname is the heaviest stone the Devil can throw at a man.
♣ America

The good seek the good and the evil the evil.
♣ England

Out of a great evil often comes a great good.

❧ *Italy*

Talk of the devil and you hear his bones rattle.

❧ *Holland*

Keep company with good men and you'll increase their number.

❧ *Italy*

Tomorrow's remedy will not ward off the evil of today.

❧ *Spain*

It's an ill wind that blows no man good.

❧ *England*

Even a big donation will not get you into heaven.

❧ *Russia*

New churches and new bars are seldom empty.

❧ *America*

Break the legs of an evil custom.

✤ *Italy*

"Neat, but not gaudy," as the devil said when he painted his tail sky blue.

✤ *England*

Even the devil flees from a thrashing.

✤ *India (Bihar)*

Hard Truths—
About Everything

Make yourself a floor mat and people will wipe their feet on you.

❧ *Creole (Belize)*

I would as soon see your nose be cheese, and the cat get the first bite of it.

❧ *Scotland*

When your loincloth is on fire, it's impossible not to speak out.

❧ *India (Bihar)*

He who builds according to every man's advice will have a crooked house.

❧ *Denmark*

A hundred years hence we shall all be bald.
❧ Spain

If I try to be like him, who will be like me?
❧ Yiddish

The pope and a peasant know more than the pope alone.
❧ Italy

If they call thee reaper, wet thy scythe.
❧ Saudi Arabia

A blind man needs no looking glass.
❧ Scotland

If I wanted to become broad, I would fall down in the middle of the road and let an elephant tread on me.
❧ Hausa (Africa)

Before you beat the dog, learn his master's name.
❧ China

Don't plug your ears when you go to steal
a bell.

❧ Japan

He who will not prosper in his sleep will not
prosper when awake.

❧ Scotland

Do not call a dog while you are holding a stick.

❧ Mozambique

There is no stripping a naked man.

❧ Germany

Never watch a bonfire in a straw coat.

❧ Japan

When you see your neighbor's beard catch fire,
wet yours with water.

❧ Jamaica

It is better it should be said "Here he ran away"
than "Here he was killed."

❧ Italy

Those who have free seats at the play hiss first.

❧ China

However little you think of the elephant, you can't say it won't fill a pot.

❧ Fulani (Africa)

Shrimps get broken backs in a whale fight.

❧ Korea

A snake that you see does not bite.

❧ Mozambique

Despise your old shoes when you get your new ones.

❧ Scotland

The barber learns to shave on the orphan's face.

❧ Saudi Arabia

Don't look for a sea when you can drown in a puddle.

❧ Russia

Even a frog would bite if it had teeth.

❧ *Italy*

If you go to sleep with the blind, you'll
awaken squinting.

❧ *Bulgaria*

A nod's as good as a wink to a blind horse.

❧ *Scotland*

A red-nosed man may not be a drunkard, but he
will always be called one.

❧ *China*

All are not free who mock their chains.

❧ *Germany*

Take down a rogue from the gallows and he
will hang you up.

❧ *France*

Stand far from dwarfs, for God has hit them on
the head.

❧ *Armenia*

As if it weren't bad enough to fall, the ladder lands on top of you.

❧ Malaysia

Bury truth in a golden coffin, it will break it open.

❧ Russia

Do not be breakin' a shin on a stool that's not in your way.

❧ Ireland

Hope is an egg, of which one man gets the yolk, another the white, and a third the shell.

❧ Denmark

On a dead tree there are no monkeys.

❧ Mozambique

Don't use oiled paper to wrap up fire.

❧ China

Even the prettiest shoe makes a sorry hat.

❧ Japan

He who would have no trouble in this world
must not be born into it.

❧ Italy

Throw him into the river and he will rise with a
fish in his mouth.

❧ Arabia

All are not asleep who have their eyes shut.

❧ Germany

Nothing falls into the mouth of a sleeping fox.

❧ Spain

The dog may bay, but still the moon stands
steady as before.

❧ Italy

You will hate a beautiful song if you sing
it often.

❧ Korea

A small leak will sink a great ship.

❧ Scotland

You cannot sew buttons on your
neighbor's mouth.

❦ Russia

There is no tattoo without blood.

❦ Mozambique

A great liar must have a good memory.

❦ Italy

The colander said to the needle,
"Get away—you have a hole in you."

❦ India

The world is a corpse and those who seek it
are dogs.

❦ Saudi Arabia

He must have clean fingers who would blow
another's nose.

❦ Denmark

At the foot of the lighthouse, it is dark.

❦ Japan

He who is an ass and thinks himself a stag
finds his mistake when he comes to leap
the ditch.

❧ *Italy*

The worst cow in the fold lows the loudest.

❧ *Scotland*

He who holds the ladder is as bad as the thief.

❧ *Germany*

Look not at thieves eating meat, but look at
them suffering punishment.

❧ *China*

He that would eat the kernel must crack
the nut.

❧ *France*

He who builds by the roadside has
many surveyors.

❧ *Italy*

Everybody who wears spurs isn't a jockey.

❧ *Martinique*

He who is his own teacher has a fool for
a pupil.

♣ *Germany*

Never put your finger between the tree and
the bark.

♣ *France*

The dog's kennel is no place to keep a sausage.

♣ *Denmark*

You cannot dance well on only one leg.

♣ *Mozambique*

He who lies down with dogs will get up
with fleas.

♣ *England*

Near putrid fish you will stink.

♣ *China*

He who puts himself between the onion and the
peel goes forth smelling like an onion.

♣ *Saudi Arabia*

Call me not olive till you see me gathered.

❦ Italy

He who blows in the fire will get sparks in
his eyes.

❦ Germany

From snow, whether cooked or pounded, all
you'll get is water.

❦ Italy

He who lets another sit on his shoulder will
soon have him on his head.

❦ Germany

When the tree is down, everyone runs to it with
a hatchet to cut wood.

❦ Italy

One bad goat will spoil the herd.

❦ Africa

The teeth freeze when the lips perish.

❦ Korea

He who has a handsome wife, a castle on the frontier, or a vineyard on the roadside is never without war.

🌸 *Spain*

Flattery is sweet food for those who can swallow it.

🌸 *Denmark*

No one puts his finger back where it was once bitten.

🌸 *Gikuyu (Africa)*

The herb patience does not grow in every man's garden.

🌸 *Denmark*

Poor men's money and cowards' weapons are often flourished.

🌸 *Italy*

He who gives away what he has before he is dead, take a mallet and knock that fool on the head.

🌸 *Spain*

Never speak of a rope in the house of one who
was hanged.

❧ *France*

Where the wolf gets one lamb, it looks for
another.

❧ *Spain*

No man is a hero in the eyes of his valet.

❧ *France*

Wash a dog, comb a dog—still, a dog remains
a dog.

❧ *France*

No one can see further into another than
his teeth.

❧ *Denmark*

When everyone says you are an ass, bray.

❧ *Spain*

A blind cat catches only a dead rat.

❧ *China*

There's no turning a windmill with a pair
of bellows.

❖ Italy

Misfortune comes on horseback and goes away
on foot.

❖ France

This is better than the thing we never had.

❖ Ireland

A goose, a woman, and a goat are bad
things lean.

❖ Portugal

A bad workman never finds a good tool.

❖ France

Even a monk can't shave his own head.

❖ Korea

Glow worms are not lanterns.

❖ Italy

You can't judge of the horse by the harness.

❧ England

The goose goes so often into the kitchen till at last she sticks to the spit.

❧ Denmark

Better to lose the wool than the sheep.

❧ Portugal

It is hard to be high and humble.

❧ England

When you buy beef, you buy bones; when you buy land, you buy rocks.

❧ Jamaica

A lion growls not in a den full of straw but in a den full of meat.

❧ Hebrew

No one is so liberal as he who has nothing to give.

❧ France

If you hit my dog, you hit myself.

❧ *Ireland*

All are not hunters who blow the horn.

❧ *France*

The headache is mine and the cows are ours.

❧ *Portugal*

Shrouds are made without pockets.

❧ *Yiddish*

Keep a thing seven years and you'll find a use for it.

❧ *Scotland*

When you point your finger at another person, look at where the other fingers point.

❧ *Jamaica*

No one can be caught in places he does not visit.

❧ *Denmark*

Baa when in a sheepfold, but in a buffalo
pen moo.

❦ Malaysia

A man who falls into a well will seize even the
edge of a sword.

❦ Hausa (Africa)

He that hath a head of wax must not approach
the fire.

❦ France

When the pig has had a bellyful, it upsets
the trough.

❦ Holland

The mosquito is little—but when he sings, your
ears are full of him.

❦ Mauritius

In the end, all foxes meet at the furrier's.

❦ Italy

What is sport to the cat is death to the mouse.

❦ Germany

Of what use is a torch at midday?

✤ *Hebrew*

He who waits for a dead man's shoes is in danger of going barefoot.

✤ *France*

One person's house burns that another may warm himself.

✤ *India*

The stone that everybody spits on will be wet at last.

✤ *Denmark*

When a flea has money, it buys its own dog.

✤ *Jamaica*

Everyone must row with the oars he has.

✤ *Germany*

While keeping a tiger from the front door, the wolf enters in at the back.

✤ *China*

The dog's tail, even if buried for twelve years, will remain as crooked as ever.

🌺 *India (Bihar)*

The well gives, but the bucket refuses.

🌺 *Hausa (Africa)*

He's like the smith's dog—so well used to the sparks that he'll no burn.

🌺 *Scotland*

A donkey is potbellied no matter how you cinch him.

🌺 *Spain*

The sting of a reproach is the truth of it.

🌺 *England*

If you would shoot a general, shoot his horse first.

🌺 *Japan*

Don't send a little boy to do a man's job.

🌺 *Creole (Belize)*

He that hunts two hares will catch neither.

❧ France

Tears are a language, but only he who weeps understands them.

❧ Armenia

Beware of a silent dog and still water.

❧ England

Rumors can come through a crack in the window.

❧ Russia

The tongue is not steel, yet it cuts.

❧ Romania

At digging time only one man will turn up; at harvest time there is no limit to the number of helpers.

❧ Maori

At the moment of birth my head was squeezed.

❧ India (Kashmir)

He who cannot dance declares that the ground is wet with rain.

❧ *Malaysia*

He who slaps himself on the face should not cry "Ouch!"

❧ *Lebanon*

Don't climb a tree to catch a fish.

❧ *China*

Barefooted folks shouldna tread on thorns.

❧ *Scotland*

When a bull begins to paw the earth, you had better look for a tree.

❧ *Jamaica*

Never wear mourning before the dead man's in his coffin.

❧ *Creole (Louisiana)*

Trouble tree don't bear no blossoms.

❧ *Virgin Islands*

Legal Briefs

Never stand before a judge or behind a donkey.
❧ *India*

Hell and the courtroom are always open.
❧ *America*

From confessors, doctors, and lawyers, do not conceal the truth of your case.
❧ *France*

Of three things the devil makes a salad: lawyers' tongues, notaries' fingers, and a third that shall be nameless.
❧ *Italy*

A lawyer and a cartwheel must be greased.

❧ *Germany*

Lawyers and painters can soon change white to black.

❧ *Denmark*

He that loves law will soon get his fill of it.

❧ *Scotland*

A lawyer's fee and a harlot's wages are paid in advance.

❧ *India*

A clever person never goes to court, and a fool never gets out of court.

❧ *Russia*

A good lawyer is a bad neighbor.

❧ *France*

He who is guilty believes that all men speak ill of him.

❧ *Italy*

The lawyer's pouch is a mouth of Hell.

❧ *France*

No sooner is a law made than a way around it is discovered.

❧ *Italy*

A golden handshake convinces even the most skeptical judge.

❧ *Russia*

The law says what the king pleases.

❧ *France*

A lawyer looks at you with one eye, but he looks at your pocket with two.

❧ *Jamaica*

'Tis better to be condemned by many doctors than by one judge.

❧ *Italy*

New lords, new laws.

❧ *England*

Truth is the best advocate.

America

Law's a deadly distemper among friends.

Scotland

Before God, be righteous; before a judge,
be wealthy.

Russia

"Virtue in the middle," said the Devil when
seated between two lawyers.

Denmark

No good lawyer ever goes to law himself.

Italy

The good lawyer knows the law, the clever one
knows the judge.

America

Unless Hell is full, no lawyer will ever be saved.

France

A peasant between two lawyers is like a fish
between two cats.

    ❧ *Catalonia*

He wastes his tears who weeps before the judge.

    ❧ *Italy*

It's an ill cause that a lawyer thinks shame of.

    ❧ *Scotland*

A bad compromise is better than a
good lawsuit.

    ❧ *France*

The priest's friend loses his faith, the doctor's
his health, and the lawyer's his fortune.

    ❧ *Italy*

Of ten reasons that a judge may have for
deciding a case, nine will be unknown to men.

    ❧ *China*

Law's costly—take a pint and agree.

    ❧ *Scotland*

You may go to court in a suit—and come out
without pants.

❧ *Russia*

Lawsuits consume time, money, rest,
and friends.

❧ *Romania*

He that buys the office of magistrate must of
necessity sell justice.

❧ *Italy*

A silent man's words are not brought
into court.

❧ *Denmark*

Lawyers' gowns are lined with the willfulness
of their clients.

❧ *Italy*

He who would win a lawsuit must have three
sacks—one filled with briefs, one with gold,
and one with luck.

❧ *Germany*

Laws catch flies and let hornets go free.

♣ *America*

A wise lawyer never goes to law himself.

♣ *Scotland*

A lawsuit is like a pit—whoever falls into it
sustains a financial injury.

♣ *Ghana*

Murder will out.

♣ *England*

Though you are starving to death do not steal;
though annoyed to death, do not file a lawsuit.

♣ *China*

The man who goes to law often loses an ox to
win a cat.

♣ *Romania*

God wanted to punish mankind, so he
created lawyers.

♣ *Russia*

On Wisdom and Folly

What a fool can spoil, ten wise men
cannot repair.

❧ *Yiddish*

He is so wise that he goes upon the ice three
days before it freezes.

❧ *Holland*

You cannot put an old head upon
young shoulders.

❧ *Scotland*

If I had a dog as daft, I would shoot him.

❧ *Scotland*

He is a fool that praises himself, and a madman that speaks ill of himself.

❧ Denmark

Friendship with a fool is like the embrace of a bear.

❧ Persia

It needs a cunning hand to shave a fool's head.

❧ Holland

He who sits in the shade won't take an ax to the tree.

❧ Japan

Don't even take a bath with fools, because they'll throw the soap.

❧ Italy

Wise men change their minds; fools, never.

❧ America

If you wish to succeed, consult three old people.

❧ China

Once a man has been bitten by a lion, he buys a dog.

❧ Mozambique

The tongue of a fool carves a piece of his heart to all that sit near him.

❧ England

Fools grow without watering.

❧ Italy

He's looking for the donkey while sitting on it.

❧ Armenia

They quarrel about an egg and let the hen fly.

❧ Germany

None can play the fool as well as a wise man.

❧ England

If you put a fool in a mortar and pound him, when you take him out he will be ten times more the fool.

❧ Jamaica

Don't scratch your shoe when your foot itches.

❧ *Japan*

He fled from the rain and sat down under the waterspout.

❧ *Saudi Arabia*

He would be wise who knew all things beforehand.

❧ *Holland*

The wise man is father of the fool.

❧ *Africa*

A simpleton's friendship is the plague of life.

❧ *India*

To give counsel to a fool is like throwing water on a goose.

❧ *Denmark*

An ounce of mother wit is worth a pound of school wit.

❧ *Germany*

A tough task has a head, but a foolish man cuts it in the middle.

❧ *Jamaica*

Never dispute with a fool, a proverb, or the truth.

❧ *Russia*

All complain o' want o' silver, none complain o' want o' wit.

❧ *Scotland*

You should look what you can swallow and what can swallow you.

❧ *India*

The tongue of the fool is always long.

❧ *Armenia*

A man profits more by the sight of an idiot than by the orations of the learned.

❧ *Saudi Arabia*

Were fools silent, they would pass for wise.

❧ *Holland*

Send a fool to close the shutters, and he closes them all over town.

      ❧ *Yiddish*

When the ship has sunk everyone knows how she might have been saved.

      ❧ *Italy*

A learned man without work is a cloud without rain.

      ❧ *Saudi Arabia*

Be careful how you handle scissors and fools.

      ❧ *Japan*

What a grown man sees from the ground, a boy can't see even from the top of a cotton tree.

      ❧ *Hausa (Africa)*

Learning is treasure no thief can touch.

      ❧ *India*

Drums sound loud because they are hollow.

      ❧ *India*

Fortune often knocks at the door, but the fool does not invite her in.

❧ Denmark

Man knows much more than he understands.

❧ Jewish

Even the fool says a wise word sometimes.

❧ Italy

Only a fool lets a dog break into his kitchen twice.

❧ Jamaica

Wisdom is in the head and not in the beard.

❧ Sweden

If you believe everything you read, better not read.

❧ Japan

It is better to carry stones with a wise man than accept the meal of a madman.

❧ Armenia

A fool is not afraid to lose his mind.

❧ Russia

A good answer at the right moment is worth an orchard and all its fruit.

❧ Lebanon

If you're going to dwell too much on how right you are, you'll wind up by being wrong.

❧ Jewish

That which the wise man does at first, the fool does at last.

❧ Italy

The idiot bakes snow in the oven and expects ice cream pie.

❧ America

Grind a fool in a mortar, and he says you don't mean him but the pepper.

❧ Yiddish

There's no fool like a learned fool.

❧ Italy

Anger looks in on a wise man's heart, but it abides in the heart of a fool.

❧ Scotland

From the well of envy, only a fool drinks the water.

❧ Hausa (Africa)

On Virtue and Villainy

Let wisdom and virtue be the two wheels of
your cart.

❧ *Japan*

Virtue comes not from chance but long study.

❧ *Italy*

Vices are learned without a master.

❧ *Italy*

An evil man is like a stump in the road—if
you stumble over him, you either fall down or
injure yourself.

❧ *Ghana*

The door to virtue is heavy and hard to push.

❧ *China*

Not everyone the dogs bark at is a thief.

❧ *Yiddish*

He that cheats me once, shame on him; he that cheats me twice, shame on me.

❧ *Scotland*

A lie can go round the world while the truth is getting its britches on.

❧ *America*

She claims to be respectable, but she's low enough to steal a nose stud.

❧ *India (Bihar)*

Beat the rogue and he will be your friend.

❧ *Italy*

It's better to be known as a rascal than a fool.

❧ *Russia*

The thief is sorry that he is to be hanged, not that he is a thief.

❧ *England*

Nothing's got without pains but an ill name.

❧ *Scotland*

No rogue like the godly rogue.

❧ *America*

Give a rascal more than he bargains for.

❧ *Spain*

He's the sort of man who, when he shakes hands with you you need to count your fingers.

❧ *Lebanon*

You can't straighten out a snake by passing it through a bamboo tube.

❧ *Japan*

The heart of man may be compared to a wurst; no one can tell exactly what's inside.

❧ *Jewish*

Riches add to the house; virtues, to the man.
❧ *China*

Thieves will be with us till Judgment Day.
❧ *America*

Do a man a good turn and he'll never
forgive you.

❧ *Scotland*

The man in boots does not know the man
in shoes.

❧ *England*

With the shade of virtue, vice is painted.
❧ *Italy*

The devil adds honey to your neighbor's wife.
❧ *Russia*

A thief is a thief, whether he steals a diamond
or a cucumber.

❧ *India (Bihar)*

Virtuous ten years is still not enough; evil one day is too much already.

          ❧ *China*

Great villainy is often called loyalty.

          ❧ *Japan*

Hang a thief when he's young, and he'll no' steal when he's old.

          ❧ *Scotland*

Rogues are rarely poor.

          ❧ *Italy*

Thieves don't like to see their comrades carrying the bags.

          ❧ *Martinique*

Search others for their virtues and yourself for your vices.

          ❧ *Scotland*

He can take milk out of coffee.

          ❧ *Jamaica*

Let someone else acknowledge your virtues.

♣ *Maori*

You are an honest man, and I am your uncle,
and that's two lies.

♣ *England*

Virtue is feared at court, not loved.

♣ *Italy*

War makes thieves, and peace
hangs them.

♣ *Scotland*

It's a crime if you get caught.

♣ *Russia*

After eating nine hundred rats, the cat is now
going on a pilgrimage.

♣ *India (Bihar)*

Virtue: climbing a hill; vice: running down.

♣ *China*

The burden of a lie is like a large tin of coals
burning fiercely on the head of its carrier.

❧ *Mozambique*

Willing is a good man, but able is a better one.

❧ *Virgin Islands*

A thread will tie an honest man better than a
rope will do a rogue.

❧ *Scotland*

There's many a good man to be found under a
shabby hat.

❧ *China*

A bad man in Zion City is a good man
in Chicago.

❧ *America*

On Time and Tide

If you live long enough, you will live to see everything.

❧ *Yiddish*

A day to come seems longer than a year that's gone.

❧ *Scotland*

There is a remedy for everything but death.

❧ *France*

Drop by drop wears away the stone.

❧ *Italy*

Joy and grief are a whirling wheel.
                    ❧ *India*

Time and tide will wait for no one.
                ❧ *England*

Last night I made a thousand plans, but this
morning I went my old way.
                  ❧ *China*

Misfortune, wood, and hair grow throughout
the year.
               ❧ *Germany*

As the tide rises, so does the high-water mark.
                      ❧ *Fiji*

Years know more than books.
                  ❧ *America*

What you push away from you today with
your foot, you will pick up tomorrow with
your hand.
                 ❧ *Martinique*

No one loves life like the old.

❧ *Spain*

Life, like a fire, begins in smoke and ends
in ashes.

❧ *Saudi Arabia*

A woman may be ever so old, if she catches on
fire she will jump.

❧ *Denmark*

The night washes what the day has soaped.

❧ *America*

Love makes time pass away, and time makes
love pass away.

❧ *France*

A wretched year has twenty-four months.

❧ *Lebanon*

Everything in its season, and turnips in Advent.

❧ *Spain*

If age and experience came at birth, we would have no youth or mirth.

❧ Russia

A hundred years cannot repair a moment's loss of honor.

❧ Italy

Would you live long, be healthy and fat, drink like a dog and eat like a cat.

❧ Germany

When one is dead, it is for a long while.

❧ France

Man is like a bubble of water on the ocean.

❧ India

To be for one day entirely at leisure is to be for one day an immortal.

❧ China

You speak first, you cut your teeth first.

❧ Fiji

O man, you who do not live a hundred years,
why fret a thousand?

❦ China

Do today what you want to postpone
until tomorrow.

❦ Lebanon

Time is anger's medicine.

❦ Germany

A fair day in winter is the mother of a storm.

❦ Romania

Speak not ill of the year until it is past.

❦ Italy

The opportunity of a lifetime is seldom
so labeled.

❦ America

Every flower has its perfume, every age
its needs.

❦ Armenia

Plan your year in spring, your day at dawn.
❦ China

Though the fool waits, the day does not.
❦ France

Time and the hour run through the
roughest day.
❦ Germany

Man crows like a rooster when he's young,
works like a donkey when he's an adult, and
growls like a pig when he's old.
❦ Spain

One swallow does not make a summer.
❦ Italy

Make the most of your time while you
are young.
❦ Maori

The first hundred years are the hardest.
❦ America

Age is a sorry traveling companion.

❧ Denmark

If you lie upon roses when young, you'll lie
upon thorns when old.

❧ Romania

Death makes no appointment.

❧ Gikuyu (Africa)

If youth knew! If age could!

❧ France

Time brings roses.

❧ Holland

The year has a wide mouth and a big belly.

❧ Denmark

The mind is like a clock which occasionally
needs correcting.

❧ Ghana

Time is a great storyteller.

❧ *Ireland*

Living in worry invites death in a hurry.

❧ *America*

Everything in time comes to him who knows
how to wait.

❧ *France*

An hour in the morning is worth two in
the evening.

❧ *Romania*

It is too late to cry "Hold hard!" when the
arrow has left the bow.

❧ *Holland*

The world is a ladder for some to go up and
others down.

❧ *America*

Great talents mature late.

❧ *Japan*

Time drives men more than any boss does.

❧ *Russia*

You come a day after the fair.

❧ *England*

Sleep faster—we need the pillows.

❧ *Yiddish*

Grey hairs are death's blossoms.

❧ *Denmark*

Three comforts of an old person: fire, tea,
and tobacco.

❧ *Ireland*

He who knew you when you were young will
not respect you when you grow up.

❧ *Lebanon*

The day has eyes, the night has ears.

❧ *Romania*

Everything passes, everything breaks,
everything wearies.

❧ France

You do not make an appointment with death.

❧ Kikuyu (Africa)

Life begins at forty.

❧ America

An inch of gold cannot purchase an inch of
time.

❧ China

What a person has done in a former birth will
come upon him again.

❧ India

He's an auld horse that winna nicker when he
sees corn.

❧ Scotland

On Travel and Travelers

The thousand-mile journey starts with one step.
❧ *Japan*

Cheerful company shortens the miles.
❧ *Germany*

Tap even a stone bridge before crossing.
❧ *Korea*

If anyone goes on a journey without taking your advice, you need not congratulate him on his safe return.
❧ *Lebanon*

No grass grows on a beaten road.

❧ France

He who puts up at the first inn he comes across very often passes a bad night.

❧ Italy

A hired horse and one's own spurs make short miles.

❧ Germany

The cock goes to town for only four days and returns home a peacock!

❧ India (Bihar)

It is not he who has lived the longest, but he who has traveled the farthest, who knows the most.

❧ Armenia

If you do not travel, you will marry your own sister.

❧ Mozambique

If you want to go fast, go the old road.
❦ America

To know the road ahead, ask those
coming back.
❦ China

Don't snap your fingers at the dogs before you
are out of the village.
❦ France

The nearer the inn, the longer the road.
❦ Germany

If you come back from a journey, offer your
family something, though it be only a stone.
❦ Lebanon

He who stands still in the mud sticks in it.
❦ China

If you carry treasure, don't travel at night.
❦ Japan

However bright the sun may shine, leave not
your cloak at home.

❧ Spain

Fair flowers do not remain long by the wayside.

❧ Germany

Thinking of where you are going, you forget
whence you came.

❧ Portugal

Tired feet always say the path is long.

❧ Jamaica

He who led me in the night, him I will thank
at daybreak.

❧ Mozambique

If you love your son, let him travel.

❧ Japan

Good company on a journey is worth a coach.

❧ Scotland

A rolling stone gathers no moss.

❧ Germany

If you stay at home you won't wear out your shoes.

❧ Yiddish

Pick your inn before dark, get on your road before dawn.

❧ China

We brought the baldheaded one along in order that he might instill courage, but he took off his hat and scared us instead.

❧ Lebanon

He who does not lose his way by night will not lose his way by day.

❧ Hausa (Africa)

The more you ask, the longer the way seems to be; the less you ask, the shorter your journey.

❧ Maori

A bad camp is better than a good march.

❧ *Russia*

Don't leave the high road for a shortcut.

❧ *Portugal*

What is the use of running when we are not on the right road?

❧ *Germany*

Don't expect to be offered a chair when you visit a town where the chief himself is sitting on the floor.

❧ *Ghana*

Call the bear "uncle" till you are safe across the bridge.

❧ *Romania*

He who is afraid of the leaves must not go into the wood.

❧ *Holland*

No man can paddle two canoes at the
same time.

❧ Bantu (Africa)

The stones of my native country are warmer
than the ovens of Babylon.

❧ Armenia

He who has slipped into the sea goes cautiously
alongside the brook.

❧ Finland

Every highway leads to Peking.

❧ China

Old horses don't forget the road.

❧ Japan

In a calm sea, every man is a pilot.

❧ Germany

God bless him who pays visits—and short visits.

❧ Saudi Arabia

Too much hurry, get there tomorrow; take time, get there today.

❧ Jamaica

The poor pilgrim laughs at highwaymen.

❧ Japan

Travel east and travel west, a man's own house is still the best.

❧ Holland

He who has left a rogue behind him has made a good day's journey.

❧ Germany

The world is dark even half an inch ahead.

❧ Japan

Good looking and good luck don't always walk the same road.

❧ Creole (Belize)

One foot cannot stand on two boats.

❧ China

Better to ask twice than to lose your way once.
❧ *Denmark*

He who doesn't know the road delays even the
one that does.
❧ *Kikuyu (Africa)*

He who has a trade may travel through
the world.
❧ *Spain*

Short is the road that leads from fear to hate.
❧ *Italy*

He that peeps into every bush will hardly get
into the wood.
❧ *Germany*

Choose your fellow traveler before you start on
your journey.
❧ *Hausa (Africa)*

It is a long road that has no turning.
❧ *Ireland*

Traveling by boat? Prepare to get wet.

♣ *China*

He may lie boldly who comes from afar.

♣ *France*

Were his word a bridge, it would be risky to pass over it.

♣ *Yiddish*

When in Rome, do as Romans do.

♣ *Latin*

When you are in town and you observe that people wear their hat on one side, wear yours the same way.

♣ *Armenia*

Never wear a brown hat in Friesland.

♣ *Holland*

Eternal Verities and Advice

A big nose never spoiled a handsome face.

❧ *France*

You shake in vain the branch that bears
no fruit.

❧ *Samoa*

When you are an anvil, be patient; when you are
a hammer, strike.

❧ *Saudi Arabia*

Every man to his taste, as the man said when he
kiss'd his cow.

❧ *Scotland*

You cannot tie a dog with a chain of sausages.
Jamaica

A wheel that turns gathers no rust.
Greece

The choicest morsel is eaten by the cook.
Spain

Pray for revenge, and God will turn a deaf ear.
Russia

Make yourself a sheep and the wolves will
eat you.
Italy

Rub an old woman's back and she will let you
taste her pepper pot.
Jamaica

Truth and oil come to the surface.
Portugal

Spur not a willing horse.

❧ France

Even the fool says a wise word sometimes.

❧ Italy

If an ox won't drink, you cannot make him bend his neck.

❧ China

God tempers the wind to the shorn lamb.

❧ France

Though you seat the frog on a golden stool, he'll soon jump off again into the pool.

❧ Germany

A tree's no' a mast till it's hewn.

❧ Scotland

When the cat's away, the mice will play.

❧ France

A monkey sees its fellow jump and jumps too.

❧ Nigeria

God hears things upside down.

❧ Lebanon

If you pull one pig by the tail, all the
rest squeak.

❧ Holland

The sea breeze blows the pelican the same place
he wants to go.

❧ Creole (Belize)

Never look a gift horse in the mouth.

❧ France

When a dog has money, he buys cheese.

❧ Jamaica

It is a bold mouse that makes her nest in a
cat's ear.

❧ Denmark

You are best when ye're sleepin'.

        ❧ *Scotland*

It is no use cutting a stick when the fight
is over.

        ❧ *Japan*

To a bold man, Fortune holds out her hand.

        ❧ *France*

We shall have a house without a flaw in the
next world.

        ❧ *Italy*

A word once spoken, an army of chariots
cannot overtake it.

        ❧ *China*

In the land of the blind, the one-eyed are kings.

        ❧ *France*

Darkness and night are mothers of thought.

        ❧ *Holland*

The tree does not fall at the first stroke.
❦ France

It's nae time to stoop when the head's off.
❦ Scotland

When sorrow is asleep, wake it not.
❦ Romania

Two sparrows on the same ear of corn are not long friends.
❦ France

The dog that is forced into the woods will not hunt many deer.
❦ Denmark

Never limp before the lame.
❦ France

Don't ask God to give it to you—ask Him to put you where there is some.
❦ Spain

Habit is a shirt that we wear till death.

❧ *Russia*

However hard a thing is thrown into the air, it always falls to the ground.

❧ *Hausa (Africa)*

He who would make a golden door must add a nail to it daily.

❧ *Germany*

A woman's tongue is her sword, and she does not let it rust.

❧ *France*

The fortune-teller never knows his own.

❧ *Japan*

All are not princes who ride with the emperor.

❧ *Holland*

If there were no sighing in the world, the world would stifle.

❧ *Creole (Louisiana)*

Paris was not built in a day.

❧ France

Rome was not built in a day.

❧ Italy

Moscow was not built in a day.

❧ Russia

A good tale is not the worse for being
told twice.

❧ England

It's only the shoes that know if the stockings
have holes.

❧ Trinidad

Think much, say little, write less.

❧ France

There is no pot so ugly but finds its cover.

❧ Spain

If you wish to know what most occupies a man's thoughts, you have only to listen to his conversation.

✤ *China*

There is bound to be a knot in a very long string.

✤ *Ghana*

The world is a pot, man a spoon in it.

✤ *Armenia*

When the goat goes to church, he does not stop till he gets to the altar.

✤ *Ireland*

Ever since dying came into fashion, life hasn't been safe.

✤ *Yiddish*

The needle is small, but it sews costly garments.

✤ *Romania*

A smiling face dispels unhappiness.

❧ Hausa (Africa)

A fable is a bridge that leads to truth.

❧ Saudi Arabia

By adding the tail to the trunk one makes up
the whole elephant.

❧ India

You cannot make a silk purse out of a sow's ear.

❧ England

If pride were a disease, how many would be
already dead?

❧ Italy

Proverbs of the common people are like salt
to speech.

❧ Lebanon

He that never rode never fell.

❧ Romania

Conversation is the food of the ears.
Trinidad

It's easy to throw something into the river but hard to take it out again.
Kashmir

The sieve with a thousand holes finds fault with the basket.
India (Bihar)

The mouse that has but one hole is soon caught.
France

If an elephant can be angry, so can the wood ant.
Africa

There are two sides to every story and twelve versions of a song.
Ireland

A bald man's head is easy to wash.

♣ *Scotland*

Listen to the wisdom of the toothless ones.

♣ *Fiji*

A cemetery never refuses a dead man.

♣ *Lebanon*

Many a mickle makes a muckle.

♣ *Scotland*

If everyone pulled in one direction, the world would keel over.

♣ *Yiddish*

Proverbs are the daughters of daily experience.

♣ *Holland*

Everything has an end—except a sausage, which has two.

♣ *Denmark*

Bibliography

Aller, Simeon. *The Russians Said It First*. Los Angeles: The Ward Ritchie Press, 1963.

Anderson, M. L. *The James Carmichael Collection of Proverbs in Scots*. Edinburgh: The University Press, 1957.

Ausubel, Nathan, ed. *A Treasury of Jewish Humor*. New York: M. Evans and Company, 1951.

Ayalti, Hanan J., ed. *Yiddish Proverbs*. New York: Schocken Books, 1949.

Bannerman, J. Yedu. *Ghanaian Proverbs Translated into English*. Tema, Ghana: Ghana Publishing Corporation, 1974.

Barra, G. *1,000 Kikuyu Proverbs*. London: Macmillan and Co. Limited, 1960.

Bayan, R. G. *Armenian Proverbs*. Venice: Academy of S. Lazarus, 1909.

Bohn, Henry G. *A Polyglot of Foreign Proverbs*. London: Henry G. Bohn Publishers, 1857.

Brallier, Jess M. *Lawyers and Other Reptiles*. Chicago: Contemporary Books, 1992.

Brougham, Aileen E., and A. W. Reed. *Maori Proverbs*. Auckland, New Zealand: A. H. & A. W. Reed, 1963.

Chinese Proverbs from Olden Times. Mount Vernon, NY: Peter Pauper Press, 1956.

Christian, John. *Bihar Proverbs*. New Delhi: Unity Book Service, 1986.

Cohen, Rev. A. *Ancient Jewish Proverbs*. New York: E. P. Dutton and Company, 1911.

Donald, James. *Scottish Proverbs*. London: William Tegg & Co., 1876.

Freyha, Anis. *A Dictionary of Modern Lebanese Proverbs*. Beirut: Librairie du Liban, 1974.

Grant, Bruce K. *Korean Proverbs*. Salt Lake City: Moth House Publications, 1982.

Hamilton, A. W. *Malay Proverbs*. Singapore: Donald Moore, 1955.

Hart, Henry H. *Seven Hundred Chinese Proverbs*. Stanford, CA: Stanford University Press, 1937.

Hearn, Lafcadio. *Gombo Zhebes: Little Dictionary of Creole Proverbs*. New York: Will H. Coleman, 1885.

Hislop, Alexander. *The Proverbs of Scotland*. Edinburgh: Alexander Hislop and Company, 1870.

Huzii, Otoo. *Japanese Proverbs*. Tokyo: Japanese Tourist Board, 1940.

Iomaire, Liam Mac Con. *Ireland of the Proverbs*. Grand Rapids, MI: Masters Press, 1988.

Japanese Proverbs. Mount Vernon, NY: Peter Pauper Press, 1962.

Jensen, Rev. Herman. *A Dictionary of Tamil Proverbs*. Delhi: Mittal Publications, 1988.

Junod, Henri Philippe. *The Wisdom of the Tsonga-Shangana People*. Braamfontein, Republic of South Africa: Sasavona Books, 1978.

Kikau, Eci. *The Wisdom of Fiji*. Suva Fiji: Institute of Pacific Studies, 1981.

Kin, David, ed. *Dictionary of American Proverbs*. New York: Philosophical Library, 1955.

Knowles, Rev. J. Hinton. *A Dictionary of Kashmiri Proverbs and Sayings*. New Delhi: Asian Educational Services, 1985.

Kogos, Fred. *Book of Yiddish Proverbs and Slang*. New York: Poplar Books, 1970.

Kremer, Edmund P. *German Proverbs*. Stanford, CA: Stanford University Press, 1955.

Lee, Jung Young. *Sokdam: Capsules of Korean Wisdom*. Seoul: Seoul Computer Press, 1977.

Lefter, Virgil. *Dictionary of Romanian Proverbs*. Bucharest: Editura Stiintifica, 1978.

Logan, W. McGregor. *Italian Proverbs*. London: A. Seguin, 1830.

Macarthur, Mildred Yorba. *California-Spanish Proverbs*. San Francisco: The Colt Press, 1954.

Macdonald, T. D. *Gaelic Proverbs and Proverbial Sayings*. Stirling, Scotland: Eneas Mackay, 1926.

Manuelian, P. M. *Seven Bites from a Raisin: Proberbs from the Armenian*. New York: Ararat Press, 1980.

Marvin, Dwight Edwards. *The Antiquity of Proverbs*. New York and London: G. P. Putnam's Sons, 1922.

Masello, Robert. *Of Course I Love You*. New York: Ballantine, 1993.

———. *Papa-tudes*. New York: Perigee Books, 1992.

Merrick, Captain G. *Hausa Proverbs*. New York: Negro Universities Press, 1969.

Minhas, Abdul Hamid. *National Proverbs: India*. London: Cecil Palmer and Hayward, 1916.

National Proverbs: Arabia. London: Cecil Palmer and Hayward, 1913.

National Proverbs: England. London: Frank Palmer, 1912.

National Proverbs: Italy. Philadelphia: David McKay, 1913.

National Proverbs: Scotland. London: Cecil Palmer and Hayward, 1913.

Njururi, Ngumbu. *Gikuyu Proverbs*. London: Macmillan and Company, 1969.

Petersen, Arona. *Herbs and Proverbs of the Virgin Islands*. St. Thomas, VI: St. Thomas Graphics, 1974.

Plopper, Clifford H. *Chinese Proverbs*. Peking: North China Union Language School, 1932.

Rovira, Luis Iscla. *Spanish Proverbs*. Lanham, MD: University Press of America, 1984.

Smith, William George. *The Oxford Dictionary of English Proverbs*. London: Oxford University Press, 1948.

Trusler, Rev. John. *Proverbs Exemplified*. New York: Johnson Reprint Corporation, 1970.

Visser, Margaret. *The Rituals of Dinner*. New York: Penguin Books, 1991.

Watson, G. Llewellyn. *Jamaican Sayings*. Tallahassee, FL: Florida A&M University Press, 1991.

Weingarten, Joseph A. and Naomi Vinogradoff. *Russian Proverbs*. New York: Weingarten, 1945.

Whitting, C. E. J. *Hausa and Fulani Proverbs*.
Farnborough Hants, England: Gregg
Press Limited, 1967.

Young, Colville N. *Creole Proverbs of Belize*.
Belize City: C. N. Young, 1986.